Activities
in the
Physical Sciences

by Helen J. Challand, Ph.D.

illustrations by Linda Hoffman Kimball

 CHILDRENS PRESS, CHICAGO

Library of Congress Cataloging in Publication Data

Challand, Helen J.
    Activities in the physical sciences.

    Includes index.
    1. Physics—Experiments—Juvenile literature.
2. Chemistry—Experiments—Juvenile literature.
I. Kimball, Linda Hoffman. II. Title.
QC33.C43   1984   500.2′07′8   83-26224
ISBN 0-516-00504-9

    3 4 5 6 7 8 9 10 11 12 R 90 89 88 87 86 85

86-1156
11/86
B+T
10.76

TABLE OF CONTENTS

CHAPTER 1
Chemistry

CHAPTER 2
Machines

CHAPTER 3
Electricity

CHAPTER 4
Magnetism

CHAPTER 5
Sound

CHAPTER 6
Color and Light

CHAPTER 7
Heat

Chapter 1
Chemistry

IDENTIFYING ELEMENTS BY THE FLAME TEST

When materials containing certain elements are burned, a particular color of flame will be evident. For example, potassium produces a reddish purple flame; sodium, yellow; boric acid, green; strontium, red; copper sulfate, green; lime, red-orange; and calcium chloride, violet-red.

Do this experiment over a cookie sheet or cake pan. A lighted candle set in the middle of the pan can serve as the heat source. Use small sticks with a little bit of cotton wrapped around one end. Dip the cotton first in tap water if the chemical is dry and then into the chemical to be tested. Hold this end over the flame until it ignites. Record the color for each element. If you select any material other than those listed above, be sure to research the safety of igniting the material. Chemistry books are your best source.

DEFINITIONS

chemical — an element or compound found in nature or man-made.

chemical element — one of the more than 105 simple substances that cannot be broken down further and of which all matter is composed.

GROUPING CHEMICALS

Test a variety of solutions and foods that you can find in the kitchen. Group them according to their pH—acid, alkaline, or neutral. Use litmus paper to test vinegar, ammonia, salt solution, lemon juice, alcohol, tap water, and a number of fruits and vegetables. Blue litmus paper turns red in acid, while red paper turns bluish in bases. No color change indicates a neutral. Readings will be much more specific using pH paper, which is sold with a color chart.

DEFINITIONS

acid — any of a group of chemical compounds that taste sour, turn blue litmus red, and can neutralize bases.

alkaline — containing a soluble salt or any base; will neutralize acids; alkaline chemicals turn red litmus blue.

base — a chemical compound that reacts with acid to form a salt.

litmus paper — a product made from the purple coloring found in certain lichens; used as an acid-base indicator, it turns red in acid and blue in base.

neutral — chemically inactive.

COMPARING GASES

Some gases are heavier or lighter than air. Air is a mixture of gases but the bulk of it (78 percent) is nitrogen. Blow up one balloon with air. Fill a second balloon of the same size with carbon dioxide by following directions.

Pour two inches of vinegar into a pop bottle. Add two tablespoons of baking soda and immediately pull the mouth of the balloon over the mouth of the bottle. The balloon will fill up with carbon dioxide. Tie off the balloon.

Hold the two balloons at the same height and release them at the same time. If you are outside be sure there is no wind. Which balloon reached the ground first? Which is the heavier gas?

For additional information see page 83

DEFINITIONS

carbon dioxide — a colorless, odorless gas used by plants to make food.

nitrogen — an element without color or odor. Almost four fifths of the air we breathe is composed of nitrogen.

11

CHANGING A LIQUID TO A GAS

Dip your fingers into various liquids, such as water, alcohol, vinegar, honey, etc. Wave your hand through the air, noting the temperature of your fingers as the liquid dries. Where did the liquid go? Is it still visible? Which liquid took the longest to disappear? Can you explain why?

Make a number of solutions with sugar, salt, baking powder, cornstarch, and other chemicals found in the kitchen. Pour half of each solution in saucers and the other half into small jars with caps. Set these aside for a day or two. Observe what happened to the solutions. Which liquids changed into gases? Describe the state of the chemicals in the saucers.

For additional information see page 83

CHANGING A GAS TO A SOLID

Soak one ball of cotton in a dilute solution (5 percent) of hydrochloric acid. Soak a second ball in ammonia. Use tongs to handle the cotton. Do not breathe the chemicals. Set both cotton balls in the bottom of a glass jar. They should not touch each other. Watch closely as a white cloud of particles begins to form. Slowly these particles will cling to the sides of the jar forming a salt, ammonium chloride. The gas from these two compounds has formed a solid.

12

CHANGING A LIQUID TO A SOLID

Some solutions will turn into solids when chemicals react with one another or by evaporation. Mix a small amount of plaster of paris in water until it is the consistency of thick pudding. Place your hand on the side of the container. Can you detect the heat of the chemical reaction? In a short time feel the mixture. How has it changed?

Mix two ounces of sodium carbonate (washing soda sold in grocery stores) in a glass of water. In a second glass of water add two ounces of calcium chloride. The latter is sold in hardware stores to melt ice and snow on sidewalks. Combine these two solutions in a mixing bowl. In a short time check the consistency of the combined solutions. You have made a chalky material often used to make toothpaste, limestone, and other commercial products.

What is the chemical principle involved in making concrete sidewalks and cement driveways? Where else in the field of industry are watery solutions made that become solids?

For additional information see page 83

DEFINITIONS

chemical reaction — the change in a substance when atoms join together or separate from atoms of a different substance to form another thing.

evaporation — the process of passing off in vapor or in invisible minute particles.

13

CHANGING A SOLID TO A GAS

Mothballs are made of naphthalene. This solid chemical does not melt into a liquid; rather, it goes directly into the air in the form of a gas. Can you smell the gas as it is escaping?

Measure the circumference of several mothballs with a tape measure. Use a string and then calculate the length by measuring the string on a ruler. Leave the mothballs exposed to the air for a couple of weeks. Remeasure their size. How long does it take for these solids to disappear completely?

Dry ice is a frozen gas. It also goes directly from a solid into the air, bypassing the liquid stage. Be careful. *Dry ice will burn your skin.* Handle it with heavy gloves or tongs. Set a piece in a Pyrex or metal pan. Hold a lighted match directly over the dry ice. What happens to the flame? What compound is dry ice?

For additional information see page 83

DEFINITIONS

circumference — the distance around a circle.

SPEEDING UP A CHEMICAL CHANGE

Wearing an insulated glove, hold a tablespoon of sugar over a flame until it burns. It will melt and turn brown but it will not blaze up. Repeat the experiment, only this time mix ashes in the sugar. Now the sugar will burn freely. The ash is a catalyst to hasten oxidation but does not change in form as the sugar does.

Heat is one of the most common forms of energy used to speed up a chemical reaction. Put wood chips in a metal can. Heat them on a hot plate until they are black. The wood has been changed to carbon or charcoal and mineral residue.

DEFINITIONS

catalyst — a substance that increases the speed of a chemical reaction without being used up or changed itself.

oxidation — the process by which a substance combines with oxygen.

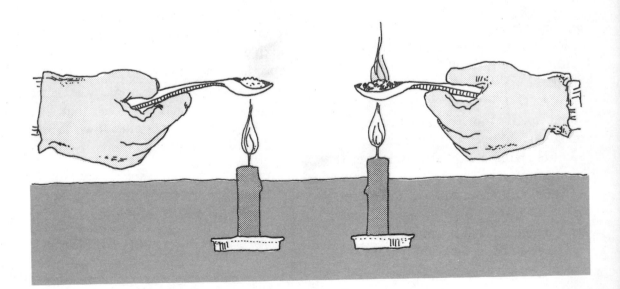

15

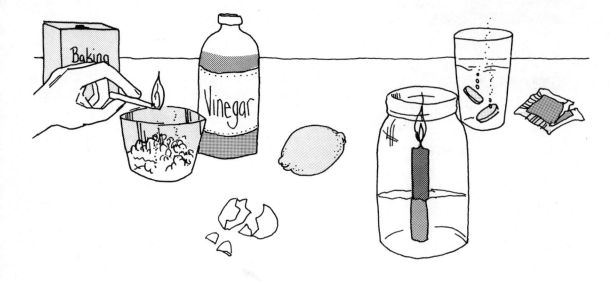

PRODUCING
CARBON DIOXIDE

Fire will not burn in air that is highly concentrated with carbon dioxide. Test the combination of two materials that release this gas.

Combine baking soda and vinegar in a cup. Light a match and hold it over the bubbling solution.

Repeat the experiment above substituting lemon juice and either lime chips, chalk, or eggshells.

Mix yeast in warm sugar water. Let it stand for five minutes. Yeast plants feed on sugar and release carbon dioxide and alcohol. Hold a lighted match over the mixture.

Put a couple of antacid tablets in a glass of water. Hold a lighted match over the glass as the chemical fizzes.

Limewater becomes cloudy when combined with carbon dioxide. Using a straw, blow air into a glass of limewater that has been filtered through a paper towel. Notice the color before and after.

Burn a candle placed in a jar with a small amount of limewater. After several minutes extinguish the flame, cover the jar, and shake lightly. The limewater becomes cloudy.

Using tongs put several pieces of dry ice in a pitcher with a few inches of water. A cloud will form since carbon dioxide gas is so cold it causes the water vapor in the air to condense. Now tilt the pitcher over a burning candle. The flame will go out. The gas is heavier than air, tumbles over the side, and down to the candle. As it surrounds the flame, oxygen is driven away.

DEFINITIONS

carbon dioxide — a colorless, odorless gas used by plants to make food.

PRODUCING OXYGEN

About 21 percent of the atmosphere is a colorless, odorless gas called oxygen, a necessary element for all living things.

Use a thermos bottle or similar container that will not break as heat is generated in these two chemical reactions. Put a tablespoon of activated charcoal in the bottle. Add hydrogen peroxide (6 percent solution sold in drugstores) until the charcoal is covered. Place a piece of paper over the opening to keep the gas from escaping. Do not screw a lid onto the bottle. Light a match or splint, then blow it out and quickly insert it into the opening of the bottle. What happens? Oxygen is a necessary element for fire.

Repeat the above experiment, substituting a small package of dry yeast for the charcoal. Did you get the same results?

For additional information see page 84

DEFINITIONS

element — one of the more than 105 simple substances that cannot be broken down further and of which all matter is composed.

oxygen — a gas without color, taste, or odor; one fifth of the air we breathe is oxygen.

EXPERIMENTING WITH OXIDATION

Oxidation occurs when other elements react with oxygen to form oxides.

Hold a small ball of steel wool underwater until is is thoroughly wet. Push it into the bottom of a small bottle. Invert the bottle and set it in a dish half full of water. Air should be trapped between the steel wool and the water. Set the experiment aside for several days before observing the changes that occur. The oxygen in the air combines with the iron in the steel to form an oxide. What color is the steel wool? What common name is applied to iron oxide? How far did the water rise in the jar as the oxygen was used up? What percent of the atmosphere is oxygen? Did your test prove this?

The chemical formula for hydrogen peroxide is H_2O_2. A 3 percent solution of this compound can be purchased in a drugstore. Put a rusty nail in a small bottle and pour in enough hydrogen peroxide to cover. Set the bottle in hot water. Notice the bubbling action. Hold a lighted match or glowing splint over the jar. What happens to the flame? What element is being separated from the compound?

Using tongs hold a spoon or coin over the flame of a candle. Soon it will have a black deposit on it. The candle is made of carbon and hydrogen. A cold object placed nearby reduces the temperature, preventing complete oxidation. The carbon, unburned, collects on the spoon or coin.

For additional information see page 84

DEFINITIONS

oxidation — the process by which a substance combines with oxygen.

RUSTING METALS

Which metals will rust or oxidize? Into a pan of water drop a brass screw, piece of tin, aluminum foil, iron nail, silver coin, gold chain, zinc plug, steel finishing nail, and a length of copper wire. Set them aside for one week. Observe and record evidences of rusting.

Select only one of the metals that oxidized. Secure duplicates of this object. Coat one with paint and a second one with oil. Cover with water. Put a third one into a copper sulfate solution. Add a fourth one to water treated as follows. Boil water to remove the air. Drop in the metal piece and add a film of vegetable oil. This will float on top and keep air from reentering the water. After a week examine these four metal pieces. What conclusions can be drawn from these experiments?

REPLACING METALS

Dissolve a few copper sulfate crystals in half a glass of water. Drop several iron or steel screws in the solution. Observe the slow accumulation of metal on metal.

Place a piece of fresh aluminum foil in soapy water overnight. Next day note its dull color. Sandpaper will clean off the oxide coating.

For additional information see page 84

19

MAKING NEW MATERIALS FROM OLD

A chemical change occurs when materials are combined to make a product that has entirely different properties from the original materials.

Heat a slice of bread in a toaster or oven until it is black. What is the name of the black material? Mix two tablespoons of vinegar in a cup of milk. What formed? Rub egg over a silver spoon. After an hour the spoon will become tarnished. Cover a silver coin with sulfur till the coin is black. Put iron filings in a jar. Sprinkle them with water. In the presence of moisture iron combines with oxygen to form what? Heat sugar until it is brown. What do you call this compound now? Combine water, iron sulfate, and tannic acid. Use this new chemical to write a letter to a friend.

For additional information see page 84

MAKING AN EMULSION

Mix a teaspoon of liquid detergent in a glass of water. Do not add anything to a second glass of water. Cut a piece of string or cord into little bits. Drop half of them into each glass. Observe and explain the results. How does this action clean soiled clothes in a washing machine?

Mayonnaise is an emulsion. Pour one-fourth cup of vinegar and three-fourths cup of vegetable oil into a jar. Shake well and let stand for several minutes. What happens to the oil and vinegar? Separate the yolk from the white of an uncooked egg. Add only the white of the

---

DEFINITIONS

emulsion — a mixture of liquids in which tiny drops of one liquid stay together and do not dissolve.

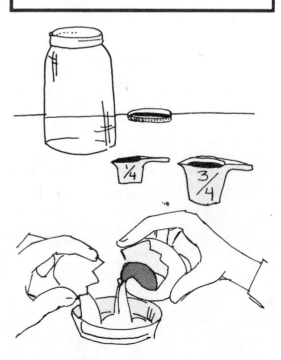

egg to the oil and vinegar. Shake again. What is the condition of the solution now? This is an emulsion.

Bile, the chemical secreted by the liver, is an emulsifier. Do some research on the digestive system to find out what food products it works on. What happens when the gallbladder is removed and the body can't store up this helpful emulsifier?

For additional information see page 85

MAKING A PRECIPITATE

Dissolve one or two small lime tablets in a glass of cold water. Keep weak lime solution off your skin. Filter the milky solution with a funnel lined with filter paper or paper toweling. Do the following within half an hour, since carbon dioxide in the air will recloud the clear liquid coming through the filter. Divide the resulting clear limewater into two portions. To one, add a little fresh carbonated water. The white precipitate formed is calcium carbonate.

Dissolve half a teaspoon of Epsom salts (magnesium sulfate) in a test tube half full of water. Add a little household ammonia (ammonium hydroxide) and the solution becomes white and opaque. A precipitate of magnesium hydroxide has formed. Aluminum hydroxide can be precipitated using alum and ammonia in the same way.

DEFINITIONS

opaque — not clear or transparent. Light cannot pass through an opaque object.

precipitate — a solid substance separated from a liquid substance.

WATCHING ATOMS SPLIT

Make sure you have a strong enough magnifying glass. Hold the glass up and look through it at your finger. If your finger is in clear focus when it is less than one inch from the glass, the glass is strong enough.

Wait until after dark for this activity. Turn out the lights in a room and wait five minutes for your eyes to adjust. Hold the magnifying glass near your eye and look at a clock with a luminous dial. Move the glass around until the dial of the clock is in clear focus. You will see sparks or flashes from the dial. The luminous paint contains radiothorium. Atoms of radiothorium are constantly splitting and particles are shooting out from them. When the particles strike the zinc sulfide in the paint, they light up. You are actually watching atoms split, although you cannot see the tiny atoms themselves.

REMOVING THE SALT FROM WATER

Locate a rubber stopper and a Pyrex or metal container that can be placed over a source of heat. Fasten a two-foot length of rubber tubing to a short glass tube and insert this into a one-holed stopper. Mix a tablespoon of salt with a pint of water and pour this into the container. Feed the other end of the tube into a bottle that is in a bucket of chipped ice. Boil the salt water until none is left. What remains in the container while the water has turned to steam? The steam can escape only through the rubber stopper hose. What happens when it hits the cool air in the bottle? Taste the water. Is it salty?

DESIGNING pH INDICATORS

The acid-base indicator used constantly in working with chemicals is litmus paper. Litmus paper indicates whether a substance is an acid or the opposite of an acid—a base. Blue litmus turns red in acid and red litmus turns blue in a base. Make a similar acid-base indicator using juice from a red cabbage.

Chop a few dark leaves of red cabbage. Cover them with water in a pan and boil for about twenty minutes. The water should be purple when you are through. This is neutral cabbage juice. Put some in a bottle labeled "neutral." To half of the rest of the juice add a small amount of baking soda. The juice will turn green. Label that bottle "basic." Add a small amount of vinegar to the other half and label the resulting red juice "acid."

To test how this indicator works, add a small amount of ammonia or baking soda (both are bases) to some of the basic indicator in a test tube. The color should stay the same. Add a little to some of the acid indicator. It should change from red to green. Now add a little lemon juice to some of the acid indicator. The color won't change. Add a little to some of the basic. Its color will change from green to red.

Test some of the following substances (in water) with your indicator: orange, tomato, onion, celery, rhubarb, salt, chlorine bleach, alcohol, cottage cheese, aspirin, starch, pickle juice, boric acid, and soap. Think of other substances to test. Be sure to record what you discover.

After using a red-cabbage indicator to test various foods, try making indicators using some of these plant parts: grape juice, rhubarb stalks, red petunias, violets, and cherries. Crush the plant parts, stir, and boil until the water is colored.

DEFINITIONS

acid — any of a group of chemical compounds that taste sour, turn blue litmus red, and can neutralize bases.

base — a chemical compound that reacts with acid to form a salt.

23

CALCULATING THE SPECIFIC GRAVITY OF MATERIALS

Pour an inch of mercury into a test tube or slender glass jar. Add an inch of water and of oil. Cap the top and shake the solution vigorously. Let it settle. What happens? Which is heavier—mercury, water, or oil? Perform an additional test. Drop into the bottle a silver dime, a block of elm, maple, or similar wood, and a cube of balsa. Observe how far down each material goes before it settles.

Do not get any mercury on your skin.

For additional information see page 85

PROVING MOLECULAR MOTION

Place four glasses of water on a table where they can remain for two days without being disturbed. Put a cube of sugar in one, a piece of rock salt in another, a tablet of vegetable dye in a third, and a piece of hard candy in the last. Do not stir the liquids. What happens to each material? Taste the two glasses containing the sugar and the salt. What color is the water in the other two glasses?

For additional information see page 85

CHECKING THE BUOYANCY OF FLUIDS

Some objects will float and others will sink in water. Have you ever floated on water in a swimming pool or lake? What is in life jackets to keep you buoyant?

Fill a large bowl or pan almost full with tap water. Drop a variety of objects into the water and record their positions in the pan. Try balsa wood, a piece of oak, rubber ball, golf ball, different sized rocks, mothball, paper clip, and cork.

Blow up a balloon. Push it to the bottom of the water. Can you feel the buoyancy of the water?

Use a spring scale to make more accurate measurements. Tie a string around a rock with one end of the string looped on the hook of a spring scale. Record the amount the rock weighs in the air. Submerge the rock into the pan of water and record this new weight. Has the rock lost weight? What is the factor that makes the difference?

Repeat the experiment with different fluids. Instead of water test the buoyancy of oil, milk, sugar water, or salt water. Increase the amount of salt in the water until no more will dissolve. Weigh the rock again. Would it be easier to float in an ocean or a lake?

Does the shape of an object affect its buoyancy in water? Cut two twelve-inch squares of aluminum foil. Crush one piece into a tight wad, leaving the second piece in sheet form. Set both in a pan of water. What happens? Does shape as well as weight affect buoyancy?

For additional information see page 85

DEFINITIONS

buoyancy — the ability to float.

DETERMINING THE DENSITY OF FLUIDS

Locate a number of uniform bottles. Baby food jars will work well. A fairly accurate weighing scale is needed for this experiment, such as a balance, kitchen, or infant scale. Select a variety of fluids: water, cooking oil, alcohol, syrup, milk, fruit juice, etc.

Begin by weighing a jar. Before weighing any liquids make some predictions. List the liquids in sequence from the lightest to the heaviest or most dense.

Now fill each jar with a different liquid to the exact same height or volume. Weigh and record each liquid and subtract the jar weight. Graph results in order of their density. How close were your predictions?

SEPARATING MIXTURES

A mixture is a combination of at least two elements or compounds. It is a physical and not a chemical combination. Mix a tablespoon each of sand and salt together. How can you tell that they are not chemically combined? Figure out a way to separate these two compounds. Can you use water to do it? Next get rid of the liquid so you end up with two neat little piles, one of sand and one of salt.

Now mix a tablespoon of iron filings with a tablespoon of sugar. Separate the two compounds by using a form of energy. What will pick up such metals as nickel and iron but not copper and lead?

Make a mixture of equal parts of buckshot and cork bits. Figure out a separation technique that will take less than a minute to do.

For additional information see page 85

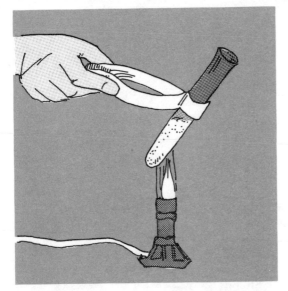

$$
\begin{array}{l}
HC=O \\
HC-OH \\
HO-CH \\
HC-OH \\
HC-OH \\
H_2C-OH
\end{array}
$$

Heat a tablespoon of sugar in a test tube over a flame. A sugar molecule is composed of three elements—six atoms of carbon, twelve atoms of hydrogen, and six atoms of oxygen. Can you break sugar apart? What element is the black residue now in the test tube? Observe the sides of the test tube. What elements are left to form this simple and most common compound?

Hold one corner of a metal pan over a lighted candle until dark particles cling to the surface. What element in the burning wax has coated and collected on the pan? Wax is an oil and fats are made of carbon, hydrogen, and oxygen. Which element did you pick?

For additional information see page 86

SEPARATING COMPOUNDS

Chew an unsalted or dietetic cracker for several minutes until it tastes sweet. What catalyst in saliva converts the complex starch molecules into simpler sugar compounds?

27

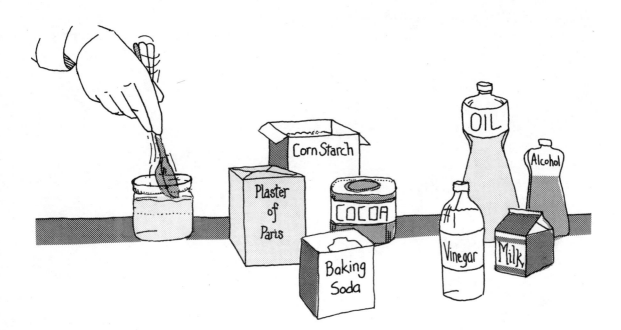

INVESTIGATING THE SOLUBILITY OF COMPOUNDS

What materials will dissolve in water? Select a variety of chemical compounds: salt, flour, sugar, cornstarch, instant coffee, vegetable oil, cocoa, baking soda, plaster of paris, bath powder, etc.

Collect a number of small glass jars. (If one jar is used it must be washed after each test.) Put one teaspoon of each material into half a cup of tap water. Stir or shake a capped jar for one minute. Record results. Which compounds were the most soluble? Which ones would not dissolve at all?

Vary this experiment by changing the solvent. Use alcohol, vinegar, milk, or lemon juice instead of water. Which solvent dissolves the most solutes?

For additional information see page 86

DEFINITIONS

solubility — the ability of any substance to dissolve in any liquid.

solvent — the substance into which other substances can be dissolved.

MIXING COLORED PIGMENTS

Either water colors or oil paints may be used for this experiment. The object is to mix two different colors to determine the color of the resulting mixture. Mix the same amount of yellow pigment to an equal amount of blue pigment. What color is it now? Try a combination of red and blue pigments, then red and yellow. Save each mixture. Blend a small quantity of two of these together to obtain still another color. Record the results each time and draw conclusions.

Does there seem to be a pattern to pigment combinations? You will find that, unlike experiments that combine colored lights, pigment colors are subtracted by others. The color that is left is the one that is transmitted to your eyes.

DEFINITIONS

pigments — coloring matter; different paints have different pigments.

29

Chapter 2
Machines

TESTING
A WHEEL AND AXLE

Usually a wheel and axle has a large wheel attached to a smaller axle. To determine the advantage in using this simple machine, divide the radius of the wheel by the radius of the axle.

Use a hand-turned meat grinder to figure the mechanical advantage. Tie a string around a heavy weight, such as a rock or book. Use a spring scale to determine the exact weight of the object. Next tie the opposite end of the string to the screw or nut on the grinder that holds the cutting discs. Hook the spring scale on the handle. As you turn it, take a reading of the amount of force needed to lift the object with a wheel and axle. What is the mechanical advantage of a meat grinder?

Examine a doorknob. The knob is the wheel and the square shaft into the door is the axle. How many times harder would it be to open a door by just turning the axle? What about steering a car or a power boat? Can you mathematically figure the mechanical advantage of a wheel and axle?

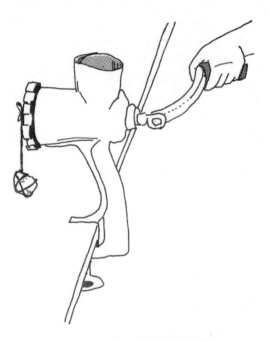

Drag a box along the floor. Feel the drag and friction involved in this action. Set two dowel rods under the box and pull it again. Did it take less work? In this case the wheel and axle had the same radius.

MEASURING THE EFFECT OF AN INCLINED PLANE

An inclined plane is simply a sloping surface that makes the work of moving heavy loads easier. You can measure how much this simple machine can help. Attach the hook of a spring scale to the axle of a toy car. Lift the car straight up off the floor to the height of a desk. Read the scale. This will tell the weight of the car and how much work you needed to lift it without the help of a machine. Now place one end of a board on the floor and the other end on the desk. Pull the same car up the sloping board and read the scale as you are pull-ing. It may be easier to use an inclined plane, but what are you sacrificing in the process? Vary the distance or angle of the plane. Can you figure out a ratio of slope versus effort needed to move an object up it?

The length of an inclined plane divided by its height gives the mechanical advantage. The weight of the body divided by the mechanical advantage is equal to the pounds of force needed to reach the top of a ramp. Compare this with the amount of force needed to climb the same height straight up a ladder. Use your own weight and an inclined plane to determine how much force is exerted and how much work was accomplished.

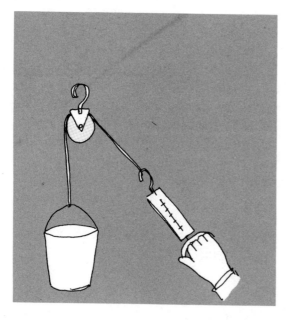

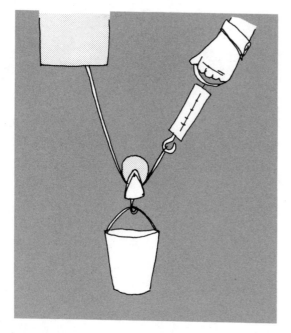

WORKING WITH FIXED AND MOVABLE PULLEYS

Purchase several small pulleys from a hardware store or science supply house. Pulleys come with a hook attached, but you will need several hook eyes and a length of cord. Build a stand to support the pulleys. A board nailed on the top of two posts will work well. Fasten the hook eyes on the underside of this board.

Work first with a fixed pulley. Hook it to one of the hook eyes and thread the cord over the grooved wheel of the pulley. Weigh a pail of water and record the weight. Tie one end of the cord to the handle of the pail and the other end to a spring scale. Raise the pail by pulling on the spring scale. Record the force needed to raise it. Compare the effort and the weight. What is the advantage of a fixed pulley?

Set up a movable pulley by fastening one end of the cord to a hook eye and the opposite end to a spring scale. Balance the pulley in the center of the cord with a pail of water hanging from the hook on the pulley. Pull up the string with the spring scale and read the weight it takes to lift the water. What is the mechanical advantage of a movable pulley? It should be equal to the number of strands holding up the resistance.

Now try combining a fixed single pulley and a movable single pulley. What is the effort needed to lift a pail of water?

Combine a fixed double pulley and a movable double pulley. How much effort is saved by using double pulleys? The fixed pulley gives no effort advantage but here you have two movable pulleys. Each movable pulley, then, reduces your effort by how much?

Now work out the following problems. Diagram a picture of a pulley system that can lift only a fifty pound object when you need to get a hundred pound weight up on a table.

Draw a picture of a pulley system that has the mechanical advantage of five, ten, or twenty.

If you were using a movable pulley, how far would you have to pull to raise an object one foot? If you pulled the cord four feet, the object would be how high off the floor?

For additional information see page 86

WORKING WITH WEDGES

A wedge is usually two inclined planes used as cutting tools to separate an object into two pieces.

A hammer and wedge are used to split logs. Smaller pieces of wood are split with a hatchet or ax. What utensils in the kitchen and garage are wedges? What is the main difference between a wedge and an inclined plane? Which one remains stationary while the object is moved?

Does the bluntness of a wedge affect the advantage in using it? Select three one-foot lengths of 2″ x 2″ wooden boards. Take one board and by using a wedge, wood chisel, or saw, make a wedge by tapering the end into two

inclined planes each measuring three inches long. Take a second stick and make a wedge on one end that measures six inches long. Do not change the shape of the third piece. This is your control. With a hammer drive each stake into the ground, noting the amount of effort and number of blows required for each. What is the advantage of using wedges to do work?

For additional information see page 86

DEMONSTRATING
THE PRINCIPLE OF A SCREW

A screw is an inclined plane going around in circles. It reduces the amount of work but increases the distance. It is much easier but takes longer to walk up a winding road around a mountain than to hike straight up as the crow flies.

Collect several wood screws with the same diameter but with threads that vary in distance apart. Find an old piece of 2″ x 4″ wood and a screwdriver. Tap little nail holes the same depth to make it easier to start the screws. Number the screws in order from the least number of threads per inch to the greatest number. As you screw each one into the wood, count the number of complete turns made with the screwdriver until the screw is one inch into the wood. Note how hard or easy each one goes in. What can you conclude?

Now take two identical screws and screw one into the wood. Take the second one and rub the threads across a damp bar of soap or coat it with oil. Screw this one into the wood. What a difference a little lubrication makes! You have reduced the amount of what between the metal and wood fibers?

For additional information see page 86

DEFINITIONS

diameter — the length of a straight line through the center of an object.

USING A LEVER

A lever is a simple machine consisting of a plank or bar used to move heavy loads. It operates around a fixed point called a fulcrum. The distance from the weight to be moved to the fulcrum is called the weight arm and the distance from where the force is applied to the fulcrum is called the force arm. In using a lever, a small force usually is applied through a large distance to move a weight a small distance.

Place a plank on a triangular block of wood so that the fulcrum is exactly in the center. Will three books on one end of the plank balance three books of the same size on the other end? Now move the plank so the fulcrum is close to where the force will be applied at the end of the plank. Put three books at the end of the long arm (weight arm). Try to lift them by placing three books on the force arm (short arm). How many books will it take to raise the weight of three books? Now move the fulcrum so that it is close to the weight. How many books will it take to raise the weight of three books?

DEFINITIONS

fulcrum — a support upon which a lever rests to lift or push something.

CLASSIFYING
LEVER ACTION

The fulcrum of a class 1 lever is between the weight and the force. In a class 2 lever the weight is between the fulcrum and force, while class 3 operates with the force between the weight and the fulcrum. Do as many of these activities as you can and classify each lever into class 1, 2, or 3:

1. - Ride on a seesaw or teeter-totter.
2. - Pick up ice or sugar cubes with tongs.
3. - Cut a sheet of paper with a pair of scissors.
4. - Pick up a specimen with tweezers.
5. - Cut a piece of meat with a knife.
6. - Eat with a fork.
7. - Drive a post into the ground with a sledgehammer.
8. - Open a door.
9. - Pull a nail out of a board using the claws on a hammer.
10. - Throw a ball as far as you can.
11. - Sweep the floor with a broom.
12. - Move a load from one place to another in a wheelbarrow.
13. - Punch a hole in a tin can with a can opener.
14. - Break a nut with a nutcracker.
15. - Move a stone with a crowbar.
16. - Write your name with a pencil.
17. - Row a rowboat around a lake.

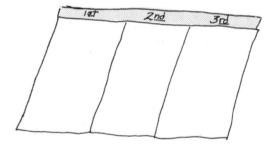

All of the devices used in these activities are levers that make work easier. Did you have trouble putting them into classes? In the last example, the weight or resistance to be moved is, of course, the boat with you in it. You are applying force on the handles of the oars. No, the fulcrum or fixed point is not the oarlock, but the water at the blade of the oar. The water seems to stand still while you push against it to make you and the boat go forward. So it is a class 2 lever.

For additional information see page 87

CALCULATING MECHANICAL ADVANTAGE OF LEVERS

The formula for the mechancial advantage (MA) of a lever is the effort arm divided by the resistance arm equals the MA. The effort end is where the force is applied and the resistance end is where the weight is resting. A lever is balanced only when the resistance times the length on one side of the fulcrum equals the resistance times the length on the other side.

Try working out the following problems to see if you understand the MA principle. Use a board and a triangular piece of wood for the fulcrum.

Using a first-class lever, place the fulcrum so that a 40-gram weight on one end balances a 120-gram weight on the opposite end. What is the mechanical advantage in this setup?

Place a 100-gram weight on one side of a first-class lever only two inches away from the fulcrum. Place a 50-gram weight on the other side at a distance so that the lever will balance. How many inches away is this latter weight from the fulcrum? What is the MA or mechanical advantage?

Work now with a second-class lever where the resistance is between the fulcrum and effort. Use a spring scale on the effort end to lift and measure the weight. A screw eye in the end of the board will let you hook on to the end of the scale. First set up the lever so that there is no mechanical advantage. Determine the weight of an object, such as a one-pound rock. Set this rock on the lever arm in a position so that it takes one pound of effort to lift the end with a spring scale. Begin to vary the distance of the weight from the fulcrum and calculate the effort needed each time to lift it. What is the greatest mechanical advantage you can get?

For additional information see page 87

DEFINITIONS

fulcrum — a support upon which a lever rests to lift or push something.

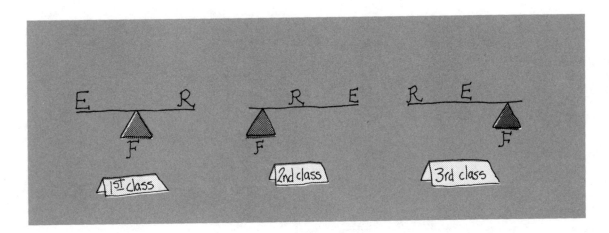

MEASURING THE AMOUNT OF FRICTION

Turn a small wagon over on its top side. Hook the end of a spring scale in the handle and pull the wagon along a level board. How many pounds of force are necessary to move it? Now put a layer of water on the board. Repeat the experiment. Did it take less force? Turn the wagon right side up on its wheels. Measure the force needed now. What does this prove?

The resistance between two moving objects is called friction. There is more friction between sliding objects than rolling ones. Water is a form of lubri-cation—it makes the surfaces smoother. This cuts down on the amount of friction produced.

Try a variety of liquids—oil, syrup, or juice—instead of water. Record the force needed to pull the wagon the same distance. Which is the best lubricant?

DEFINITIONS

friction — the force of resistance a body offers to motion, produced by its contact with another body; may be rolling friction, as with wheels or ball bearings on a surface, or sliding friction, as with a box being dragged over a surface.

ACTING AND REACTING

Many years ago a scientist named Isaac Newton proposed several theories about the principles of motion. They have proven to be so accurate that they are known as laws. Newton's third law states that for every action there is an equal and opposite reaction. Following are a number of activities to prove this law.

Blow up an elongated balloon and then release it. Which direction does the balloon go in relation to the air rushing from the opening? Explain about air pressure inside the balloon.

While standing on roller skates throw a ball to a friend. Are you still in the same spot? Now throw a fast, hard pitch.

Was there any difference in your reaction? Throw a ball straight up in the air. Did you move?

Turn on a rotating garden sprinkler. Notice the direction the sprinkler turns in relation to the squirting water.

Punch several holes around the outside of a paper cup about an inch from the bottom. Punch two holes near the top in order to tie two strings. Hold the cup under a faucet with these. Turn on the water and observe the directions the water and the cup move.

Put a doll in a toy wagon. Pull it along and then stop it suddenly. What happens to the doll? Tie a belt around the doll and fasten the belt to the wagon. Pull the wagon again and stop it. Does this help explain why you should wear a seat belt when you are riding in a car?

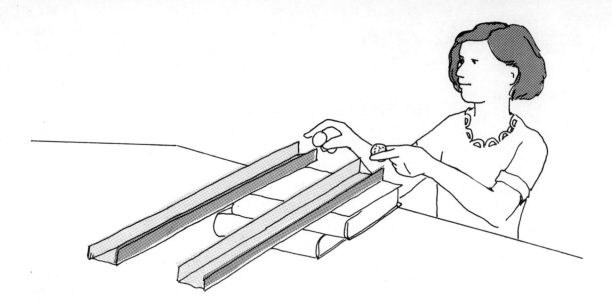

EXPERIMENTING WITH MASS AND MOMENTUM

Will any two objects the same size travel at the same speed? Set up the following experiment to find the answer.

Cut two pieces of corrugated cardboard three-inches wide by twenty-four inches long. Use a sharp knife on a hard surface so the cardboard does not bend. Cut four one-inch strips and glue them to both sides of the two long strips. You have now assembled two troughs in which to conduct a rolling experiment.

Prop one end of each trough on a book to create two small sloping runways. Hold a golf ball in one hand and a Ping-Pong ball in the other at the top of the slopes. Release the balls at the same time. Did they roll off the end of the troughs together? Repeat the activity several times. If you have a stopwatch you can get a more accurate estimate of speed for each ball. Weigh the two balls with a spring scale. Can you mathematically figure out the ratio of speed to mass?

Try the same experiment adding a book each time to increase the steepness of the slopes. Does this make a difference?

Do one more variation. Set up sloping troughs on a flat, smooth floor with several feet beyond the end of the slopes. Roll the balls again. This time see which ball rolls the longest after it is on the flat surface. Which one stopped first? What does this tell you about mass and momentum?

For additional information see page 87

DEFINITIONS

mass — the amount of matter an object has; mass can be measured in weight.

momentum — the force with which an object moves.

UNDERSTANDING INERTIA

The principle of inertia states that an object at rest tends to stay at rest even when some force is trying to move it. It also states that an object that is moving tends to keep moving, resisting the effort to stop it. Try these experiments to demonstrate this principle.

On a smooth, flat surface set a stone or brick on one side of a sheet of cardboard. Turn up one corner of the cardboard and grasp it. Pull the cardboard with a quick snap of the wrist. What happened to the object resting on top? Repeat the experiment. This time pull with a slow, steady motion. Explain the results. When you become expert at this technique, try pulling a cloth napkin out from under a full glass of water.

Set a marble on top of a small piece of cardboard over the mouth of a plastic bottle. You now have a rolling object which is more difficult to manage than a stone or brick. Pull quickly on the cardboard. How many marbles can you get into the bottle before you miss? Try a bottle with a smaller opening. Be sure the marble is directly over the hole.

Cut the top flaps off an empty cereal box. Set a tennis or golf ball inside the box. Lay the box on its side. Start pushing the box along a smooth surface, open end forward. After you have picked up a little speed stop the box. What happened to the ball? Put the ball in the box and this time push it quickly with the closed end forward. Where is the ball now?

For additional information see page 87

41

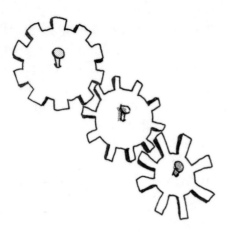

Experiment with the different sizes. What happens when you turn a four-inch wheel that connects with the teeth of a two-inch wheel? In which direction do they move? Place a little dot on the edge of each wheel to help count a single rotation. If you make one turn with the large wheel, how many rotations did the smaller wheel make? What are the two advantages of having gears on cars, bicycles, and similar complex machines?

For additional information see page 87

WORKING WITH GEARS

A gear is a wheel with teeth. Make several sized gears out of balsa wood, which is easy to cut with a sharp knife. Always cut away from the hand holding the wood. If it takes too long to cut a wheel and gears from one piece, draw circles and cut the wheels separately. Then cut a long narrow strip into small, equal pieces. These "teeth" can be glued onto the outer circle of the wheel. Be sure to space them so that a gear from one wheel can mesh with (fit in between two gears of) another wheel. It will be easier to calculate later if your wheels have a radius that is divided by or multiplied by the same number. For example, the radius of a set might be two, four, six, and eight, or three, six, nine, and twelve.

Drive a nail through the exact center of each wheel, then into a wooden base so that the teeth will mesh with each other. Be sure the wheels rotate around the nail with the least amount of friction.

DEFINITIONS

radius — straight line from the center of a circle to the outside of a circle.

rotate — turn on its axis; the earth rotates on its axis and produces day and night.

DEMONSTRATING BELT-DRIVEN MACHINES

Collect four different-sized, empty spools that once held sewing thread. Record the radius of each spool. Push a thumbtack into the top of each spool near the edge. The tack can be used to note one rotation. Cut an eight-inch-square board to serve as a base. Hammer a long nail into each corner of the base. Set a spool on each nail. Loop a rubber band around two of the spools. Turn the larger spool one full turn. How much did the smaller wheel rotate? In what direction did it turn in relation to the larger wheel? Can you figure out how to make the smaller wheel go in the opposite direction?

Experiment with all four wheel sizes. Use several rubber bands. Calculate the rotations as to size. Can you figure out a ratio that would work with even larger or smaller spools than the ones available? Look under a hood of an automobile. Ask a garage mechanic to explain what all the belts do.

DEMONSTRATING BERNOULLI'S PRINCIPLE

Flying machines operate, in part, on the principle of the difference in air pressure. Here are two activities you can do to understand this concept.

Suspend two tennis balls on long threads from a door frame or other firm support. Using a bicycle pump, direct a blast of air between the two balls. What happens to the position of the balls?

Hold a thin sheet of paper in front of your lips and blow across the top surface. Does the paper move up or down? Compare this to a wing of a plane as it moves through the air at great speed.

Bernoulli's principle—that where velocity is high, pressure is low—is one of the basic principles involved in aircraft flight.

For additional information see page 88

DEFINITIONS

radius — straight line from the center of a circle to the outside of a circle.

ratio — a proportion; the quotient of one physical measure divided by another of similar units; always a number with no dimension; a percentage is a ratio.

rotate — turn on its axis; the earth rotates on its axis and produces day and night.

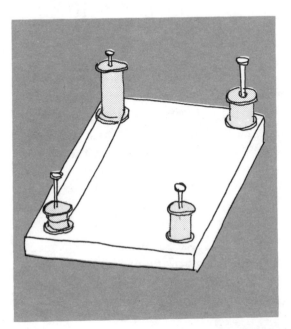

DEFINITIONS

velocity — the rate of motion (speed) of a body in a given direction; velocity equals distance divided by time.

Chapter 3
Electricity

PRODUCING A CHARGE WITH FRICTION

1. On a cold, dry day shuffle your rubber-soled shoes back and forth on a wool rug. Step over to a metal part on a stove or radiator and quickly tap it with your finger. What happens between the two objects?

2. Comb the fur of a cat rapidly with a rubber comb. If the day is really dry, watch the fur.

3. Blow up a balloon and tie it. Rub it on the sleeve of a woolen sweater. Touch the balloon to a wall and let go of it. Does it fall down?

4. Rub a glass rod with a silk cloth thirty times. Now hold the rod close to a small stream of water coming from a faucet. What happens to the path of the water?

5. Find a fluorescent tube, a piece of wool, a balloon, and a very dark closet to do this experiment. Blow up the balloon and rub it vigorously with the wool. Quickly touch the balloon to the end of the fluorescent tube. If your eyes have adjusted to the total darkness, you should see something.

6. Hold a sheet of paper against a smooth wall. Rub it briskly with a piece of cloth. Let go of the paper. What holds it to the wall? How long will it stay there before it falls to the floor?

7. Can you make paper jump up and down? Tear a piece of paper into tiny bits. Place them into a shallow, glass-covered bowl so you can watch them. Rub the cover for one minute with a piece of nylon. Watch the paper for several minutes and explain the actions.

For additional information see page 88

INVESTIGATING A DRY CELL

Use a dry cell that is worn out. (It will be unusable when you get through studying the insides.) Remove the cardboard covering to expose the metal casing. This container is usually made of zinc and is the negative pole. Saw the cell in half lengthwise. The center core contains a carbon rod or positive pole. Between the zinc and carbon is the electrolyte, a moist paste of ammonium chloride. Because of this the cell isn't really dry, but it serves well in flashlights, clocks, and other appliances where there would be spillage if a wet cell were used.

On top of the dry cell are the two terminals. When the insides are exposed, notice that the center terminal is in contact with the carbon while the one on the edge connects to the zinc. The zinc piles up electrons while the carbon has lost electrons. Therefore, when you connect a wire from the zinc terminal to the carbon terminal, the electrons rush over to the carbon. Connect a light between the terminals and you will see this rush of electrons. Chemical energy in the cell has been changed to radiant energy.

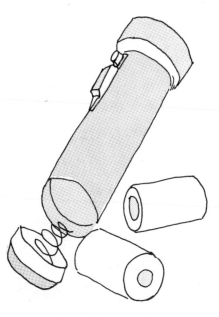

FINDING OUT HOW A FLASHLIGHT WORKS

Take apart both a flashlight with a plastic case and one with a metal case.

Examine the position of the dry cells. Would they work if you turned them upside down? How is the switch connected to the circuit of cells and bulb? What is used for insulation?

Assemble a simple flashlight by wrapping one exposed end of a piece of bell wire around the base of a flashlight bulb. While holding the bulb on top of a dry cell, bring the other end of the wire around and touch the metal on the bottom of the cell. With a switch and a case to hold this setup, you would have a homemade flashlight.

TESTING MATERIALS THAT MIGHT CONDUCT ELECTRICITY

Assemble the electrical tester before mixing any of the solutions to be used in this experiment. Connect a piece of bell wire from one terminal on a dry cell to one post on a small light receptacle. Connect a second wire to the other terminal and a third wire to the other post. Remove insulation at all contact points. Expose three inches of the free ends of the bell wire. These will be placed in a glass to test the conductivity of several solutions. If a solution is an electrolyte, the bulb will light up.

Make a solution with water and each of these materials just before the test: sugar, baking powder, baking soda, vinegar, ink, lemon juice, and apple juice. Test them separately in the circuit arrangement. When certain materials dissolve in water they will dissociate into positively and negatively charged ions. The solution will then conduct an electric current. Which solutions were good conductors?

DEFINITIONS

electrolyte — a liquid that conducts electricity.

ion — an electrified atom or molecule that has gained or lost electrons.

IDENTIFYING SOLIDS THAT WILL CONDUCT ELECTRICITY

Collect a number of items to experiment with in determining which ones will permit an electric current to flow through them.

Connect a light socket to a dry cell. Cut a piece of wire in the middle and remove the insulation from all ends. Connect one piece to the light socket and one to the dry cell, leaving about an inch between the pieces. Lay different objects across the two ends. Try cardboard, tin, an iron nail, a coin, cloth, a flat stone, a safety pin, a plastic straw, a pencil, the lead in the pencil, a steel screw, Styrofoam, aluminum foil, and a spoon. Which ones close the circuit and permit the bulb to light up?

For additional information see page 88

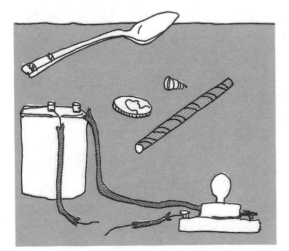

GETTING A CHARGE OUT OF A LIME

The basic parts of an electrical cell are strips of two different metals and a chemical to conduct a current. Lime juice, since it is an acid, is an electrolyte.

Purchase zinc and copper strips from a hardware or hobby store. Roll a lime in order to make it juicy inside. Insert the two strips, making sure they do not touch inside the lime. Touch the ends of both strips at the same time with your tongue. You should be able to feel a slight tingling sensation, which means a current is flowing. It is probably not enough current to be detected by a home-made galvanometer, but you can check it out and see.

DEFINITIONS

acid — any one of a group of chemical compounds that taste sour, turn blue litmus red, and can neutralize bases.

electrolyte — a liquid that conducts electricity.

USING SALT TO CONDUCT ELECTRICITY

Connect a small bulb to a dry cell with bell wire. Fasten a second piece of wire to the remaining terminal of the bulb receptacle and lead the exposed end of it to a dish of water. Connect a third wire to the other terminal of the dry cell and lead it to the dish. The two wires in the water may be an inch apart. Remove insulation from the contact points.

Does the bulb light up? Mix a tablespoon of table salt into the water. What happens now? Dissolve a second tablespoon of salt in the solution. Does the bulb burn more brightly? Continue adding salt until the solution is saturated, a point when no more salt will dissolve. This is the brightest the light will ever get—at least in this electrolyte.

For additional information see page 89

DEFINITIONS

electrolyte — a liquid that conducts electricity.

PLATING A SPOON WITH COPPER

Precious metals, such as silver and gold, are so expensive that often only a thin layer is applied to a cheaper metal for utensils, coffee services, jewelry, etc. This is done by electroplating. You can duplicate this process on an old metal spoon.

Purchase a copper strip, two dry cells (No. 6), bell wire, and copper sulfate crystals. Mix a concentrated solution of copper sulfate until it is deep blue. Use a short piece of bell wire to attach the dry cells together as shown in the picture. Attach a strip of bell wire from the positive post (marked on the dry cell and usually the center screw) to the copper strip. Attach a second wire from the negative post (screw on outer edge of the cell) to an old metal spoon. The insulation should be removed from the wire at the contact points.

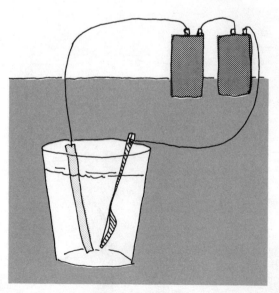

Insert the copper strip and spoon into a beaker of copper sulfate solution, making sure the two objects are not touching. A chemical reaction will occur. The copper sulfate is the electrolyte that carries the current. Copper ions (positively charged) leave the strip and become attached to the spoon (negatively charged). When the copper ions are entirely transferred you will end up with a copper-plated spoon.

Try electroplating with other metals and different electrolytes.

DEFINITIONS

electrolyte — a liquid that conducts electricity.

ion — an electrified atom or molecule that has gained or lost electrons.

DEMONSTRATING A SHORT CIRCUIT

Set up a simple electrical circuit to be shorted out. Connect a piece of bell wire from one terminal of a small light receptacle to one post of a dry cell. Connect a second wire from the other post of the dry cell to a screw on a one-way switch. Connect a third wire from the other screw on the switch back to the other terminal on the light receptacle. If you have made all connections correctly, the light will burn if the switch is in a closed position. Did you remember to strip the wires of insulation at all the connecting points?

Disconnect the circuit and remove the insulation from places on two of the wires. Lay the metal part of a screwdriver across the two bare places and reconnect the circuit. In this case the current flows over the screwdriver rather than through the lamp. The bulb may still get some electrons but will be very dim. Feel the screwdriver after a few minutes. What form of energy has electricity been turned into?

In place of the screwdriver use water. Place the two bare sections of wire close together but not touching in a shallow dish of water. What happens to the light? Where is the electricity going? Does this explain how people get electrocuted when they go into a flooded basement with old wiring and appliances plugged in underwater?

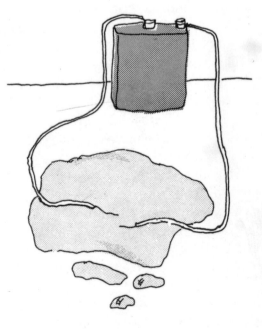

49

DEFINITIONS

voltage — amount of electrical power; can be measured in volts.

WIRING A SERIES CIRCUIT

There are three ways to wire in series. You can wire dry cells in series or you can wire lamps in series, or both.

To wire three dry cells in series, attach the outside terminal of one cell to the inside terminal of the next and so on. The total voltage supplied to the circuit is the combined voltage of all three cells. Notice the difference in brightness in a lamp when it is connected to one cell and then to two or three.

To connect lamps in series, run a short piece of wire from one screw on a lamp to a screw on the next and so on. Run a long wire from the second screw on the last lamp to the dry cell.

Unscrew one of the bulbs in the series. Do they all go out? Why? Trace the flow of electrons from one terminal of the dry cell back to the other terminal.

DEMONSTRATING THE FUNCTION OF A FUSE

Connect three dry cells in series with cut lengths of bell wire. Be sure to remove the insulation where the wire connects to the posts on the dry cells. Cut a strip of thin metal foil, one-eighth-inch wide, to serve as the fuse. Insert a pin through each end of the strip. Stick the pins with the strip into the tops of two corks. With a piece of wire, connect the first dry cell to one pin. Connect the wire from the third cell to one screw on a light socket. Run a wire from the second screw on the socket to the second pin.

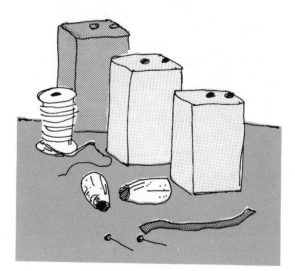

50

While the light is on, take another wire and touch the two screws on the light socket. What happens to the foil fuse? Did the circuit of electrons go in a different path? What happens to the light when you blow a fuse?

Examine a fuse used in a home fuse box. Compare it with a blown-out fuse. Find out about fuse breakers and why they can be used over and over again.

For additional information see page 89

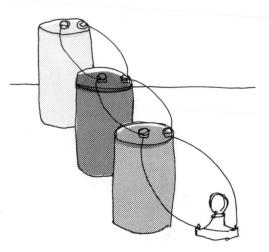

DEFINITIONS

electron — the smallest particle known to exist with a negative electric charge.

WIRING A PARALLEL CIRCUIT

There are three kinds of parallel wiring. Lamps can be wired in parallel or dry cells can be wired in parallel, or both.

Connect three dry cells in parallel by attaching all three center terminals to one wire. Scrape off the insulation at contact points. Connect all outside terminals to another wire. Connect the ends of the wires to a lamp. Disconnect one of the dry cells from the circuit. Does this affect the brightness of the light?

Wire lamps in parallel by running one wire down the side of all three sockets, making contact at the screws. Run a second wire down the other three screws in each socket. Unscrew one bulb. Do the others go out? Can you trace a complete circuit through each lamp independent of the others?

Chapter 4
Magnetism

MAKING MAGNETS

In ordinary pieces of metal the atoms are all scrambled up. In a magnet scientists think that atoms or groups of atoms line up in a definite pattern end for end. See if you can duplicate this design.

You will need a strong magnet, a test tube or similar transparent container, and tiny finishing nails to observe the action. Fill the container three-fourths full with nails. Stopper the open end. Holding the test tube at an angle, rub a magnet along the glass in the same direction about forty times. What happens to the positions of the nails? Hold a compass near one end of the tube. Does anything happen to the needle? Shake the test tube and disarrange the nails. Retest with the compass. What is the reading now?

Use a steel knitting needle or long sewing needle to make a magnet that is more permanent. Stroke one half of the needle about fifty times with the north end of a bar magnet. Stroke the other half (the eye end) the same number of times with the south end of the magnet. Tie a piece of sewing thread to the center of the needle so that it swings free as you hold the other end of the thread. Place a compass near the point of the needle. What is the reading on the compass? Now hold it near the eye end of the needle. Is this the north or south pole of your homemade magnet?

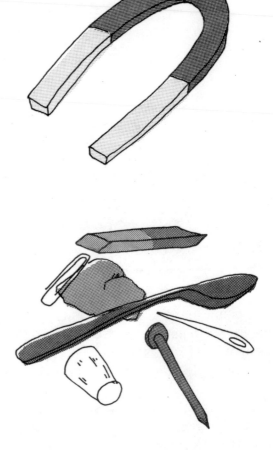

TESTING MATERIALS THAT MAGNETS WILL ATTRACT

Collect a number of objects that are made of a variety of materials. Here are a few suggestions: paper clip, thumbtack, pin, rubber eraser, plastic spoon, penny, metal slug, brass fastener, marble, iron nail, silver dollar, gold necklace, tin can, steel screw, piece of wood, aluminum foil, lead pipe, rock, sewing needle, graphite lead in a pencil, nut and bolt, cork, bottle cap, table knife, etc.

Before you do any testing with a magnet, sort your objects into three piles. Into one pile place all objects you are certain will be attracted by the magnet. In a second pile place those you predict will not be attracted. The last pile should contain objects you are doubtful about. Now test each pile, record your errors, and classify into two piles. How close were your predictions? Magnets will pick up objects only if they contain one of three metals. Two of them are not commonly found around the house or at school. Can you name them?

TESTING THE POLES OF A MAGNET

Like the earth, every magnet has a north pole and a south pole. This experiment will help you find which pole is north and which is south on a magnet. It will also help you make up rules about poles.

You probably already know that a compass needle is a magnet. The end with the arrow always points toward the north magnetic pole of the earth. On a magnet, it is also called the north pole. (More accurately, this pole of the compass needle should be called the north-seeking pole.) The other end of the compass needle is the south (or south-seeking) pole.

Place one end of a bar magnet near a compass. If the north pole of the needle is attracted to it, mark that end with an "S". If the north pole of the needle is repelled by it, mark it "N". Do this with both ends.

You have seen two north poles repel each other and you have seen a north pole and a south pole attract each other. Is this always true?

Bend a brass wire so that it forms a cradle for a bar magnet. Suspend it from a solid surface with a string. Lay one marked magnet in the cradle. Bring the pole marked "N" on a bar magnet in your hand close to the one marked "N" on the suspended one. What happens? Now bring two south poles together. Next, a north pole and a south together. Tie a string around the center of a horseshoe magnet and hold it suspended. Test its poles in the same way, using a marked bar magnet. What rule about magnets have you discovered?

PROVING THAT MAGNETISM GOES THROUGH AIR

Tie twelve-inch pieces of thread to a small paper clip and a large paper clip. You could use two finishing nails instead, if one is twice as long as the other. Tape the free end of each thread to a tabletop. While holding the small clip up in the air, bring a magnet one-half inch above it. Let go of the clip. Move the magnet back and forth. What happens to the paper clip? Pass a sheet of paper, then cardboard, and finally a sheet of metal between the magnet and clip. Can the magnetism get through each of these materials?

Repeat the same experiments with the larger paper clip. Do size and mass make a difference? Try using a stronger magnet. To test the strength of two magnets see how many paper clips each will pick up at one time. How far away from the clip can you move the magnet before you lose the attraction?

> **DEFINITIONS**
>
> **mass** — the amount of matter an object has; mass can be measured in weight.

SHOWING THE MAGNETIC EFFECT OF ELECTRICITY

Insert a length of bell wire through the center of a cardboard cylinder. Connect the two ends to the terminals of a dry cell. Hold the wire up so that the circle is horizontal above a table. Sprinkle iron filings or tiny bits of steel wool on the cardboard. Does a magnetic field form around the wire? Do not connect the wires for long, or the cell will soon be worn out.

CONDUCTING MAGNETISM THROUGH MATERIALS

You will need a fairly strong magnet and iron filings for this experiment. If you are unable to buy iron filings at a hobby shop or machine shop, make some by cutting steel wool into very fine bits.

Build a stand with two piles of three books each. Place a sheet of glass across the piles of books. Sprinkle iron filings on top of the glass and move the magnet around underneath it. Does the magnetism act through the glass? Try the same experiment using cardboard, a wooden board, aluminum foil, a sheet of plastic, and a cookie sheet in place of the glass. Do the magnetic lines of force pass through all these substances? Drop some iron filings in a dish of water. Will magnetism work underwater to attract the filings?

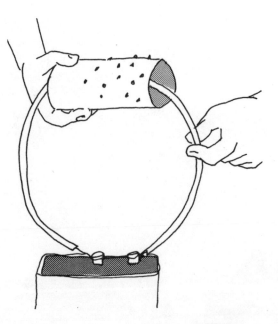

SHOWING THE STRENGTH OF MAGNETISM

Purchase two No. 6 dry cells, a knife switch, and a roll of bell wire at a hardware store. Locate a circle of Styrofoam about a half-inch thick and small enough to slip through the mouth of a pop bottle or similar glass container. Push a sewing needle through the center of the Styrofoam until the eye of the needle is even with the upper surface. Fill the bottle three-fourths full with water and drop in the needle and the Styrofoam. It should float at the top of the water.

Use just one of the dry cells first. Using bell wire connect one of the posts of the dry cell to one screw on the open switch knife. Take the rest of the roll of wire, connect one end to the other dry cell terminal, and then wind wire around the pop bottle, making at least 150 turns. Leave a little space between the wires so you do not hide the floating needle from view. Finally attach the end of the wire to the other screw on the knife switch. You should have gone full circle and are ready now to test it. Close the switch for a couple of seconds, watch the needle, and then open the switch. What happened? Add the second dry cell to the circuit and test the strength of the magnet (coil of wire) again. What if you made even more turns on the bottle? Experiment and draw conclusions.

Chapter 5
Sound

SENDING SOUND WAVES THROUGH LIQUIDS AND SOLIDS

Fill a pail or dishpan with water. Hold two rocks under the water and strike them together forcibly. Can you hear a sound?

Put your ear close to the end of a wooden table. Ask another person to scratch the wood at the opposite end with a fingernail or other sharp object. Can you hear the sound through the wood? If you can locate a metal table the same length, try it again. Is there any difference between the sounds you hear?

Would you hear a sound if there were no atoms of a solid, liquid, or even a gas through which waves can be conducted? Suspend a small bell in a jar and with a vacuum pump (often available in junior high school labs) remove most of the air from the jar. Shake the jar. Can you hear the bell ring?

Hold a watch away from your ear at the distance where you no longer can hear it. Place one end of a metal curtain rod on the watch and the other end to your ear. What has happened to the vibrations now?

PRODUCING SYMPATHETIC VIBRATIONS

Have you ever been in a house or building that is near train tracks and as a train goes by the dishes or other objects in the house will rattle? Sometimes when an airplane breaks the sound barrier the sympathetic vibrations on the ground cause damage. Likewise a loud gunshot can break an eardrum. To illustrate this phenomenon try this.

Locate two tuning forks. Strike one fork a good blow with a rubber mallet. Hold it in line with the second tuning fork. Can you see it vibrate also? If not, quickly touch the prongs to your cheek. Can you feel it now?

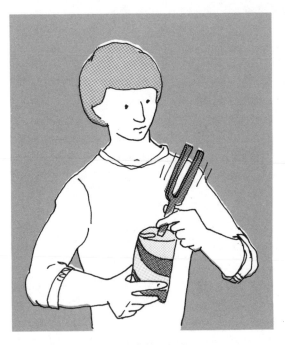

INCREASING THE INTENSITY OF VIBRATIONS

Strike a tuning fork on the rubber sole of your shoe (hard surfaces dent the fork and ruin its pitch) and listen to the vibrations. How loud is the sound? Can you see the fork vibrating after you are unable to hear it?

Place the handle of a vibrating fork against a full can of pop. What sound does it make? Place the prongs of a vibrating fork against a full can of pop. What sound does it make? Drink the pop and repeat the experiments. How does the sound change?

Strike a tuning fork again and while it is vibrating place the end of the handle on a wooden tabletop. Explain the sound. Repeat again using a metal table. How does the sound vary with the different materials?

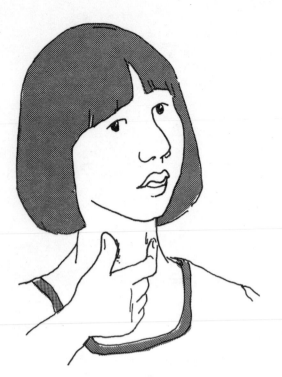

MAKING VIBRATIONS YOU CAN SEE AND TOUCH

You have a box in your body that helps you make sounds. Put your thumb and finger on the sides of your larynx or voice box in the throat. Press slightly, but not too hard, as you make a low growl like a bear. Now make a screech like an owl. Can you feel the different number of vibrations with each sound? Make each sound with your mouth open. Now close your mouth, hold your nostrils closed, and repeat the sounds. Explain the difference.

Strike a tuning fork on the sole of a rubber-soled shoe. While it is vibrating touch the end of the prongs to the surface of water in a pan. What can you see?

Obtain an old pocket mirror that is no longer needed. Wrap the mirror in cloth so that you can safely hit it with something to make it break. You need a piece about one-fourth-inch square. Cut one end off a round salt box. Then cut out a disk in the other end, leaving about an inch all the way around. Paste a circle of onionskin paper onto the rim left so that it covers the opening. Glue the small piece of mirror on the outside of the thin paper in an off-center position. Have a friend hold a flashlight so that it shines on the mirror. Hold a piece of white cardboard so that the reflected spot of light from the mirror shines on it.

Talk into the carton. The reflected ray of light will make a pattern on the cardboard as the mirror vibrates. Experiment with singing, making vowel sounds, shouting. What is the difference in pattern between high-pitched and low-pitched sounds? What about loud and soft sounds?

This instrument is similar to an oscilloscope, except that an oscilloscope shows a picture of an electrical signal made by the vibrations rather than of the sound itself.

REDUCING THE INTENSITY OF VIBRATIONS

Obtain a coffee can, cigar box, and shoe box. Line the shoe box with corrugated cardboard. Put several stones in each container. Cover each tightly and tape the lids down. Shake each container separately and vigorously. Which makes the loudest sounds?

Collect a variety of materials to check out how well they absorb sound. Try cork, rubber, wool, commercial insulation, felt paper, Styrofoam, plastic, plywood, and cotton. Set each piece on a wooden box and hit it with a hammer. Be sure to use the same amount of force each time you strike. Make a list of the materials, from the one that does the best job of muffling noise down to the poorest material for insulating against sounds.

What are some of the materials used in the design and construction of buildings to reduce the intensity of sound vibrations?

LOCATING THE DIRECTION OF SOUND

Stand outside in a busy place and listen for all kinds of sounds. Are sounds coming to your ears from the ground? Can you hear any sounds coming out of the sky down to you? What noises are to the sides, the back, and the front of you? Can you hear sounds from objects you can't see, such as a fire engine coming down the street? Does this prove sound travels around corners? Put your hand tightly over one ear. Listen again. Does this make a difference in locating the direction of sound?

EXPERIMENTING WITH PITCH

Place a meter stick or yardstick on a table so that half is off the edge. Put one hand on the stick at the edge of the table and press hard while you lift up the free end and then let it go. Listen to the sound. Move the stick until three fourths of it extends off the table. Press the stick on the table and vibrate the extended length. Listen. Is the sound higher or lower than the first time? Keep extending it out over the end. In what direction is the sound going—higher or lower?

Now use rubber bands to determine the principle of pitch. On a two-foot board hammer five nails in a row along one end. Hammer one nail at the opposite end of nail number 1. Hammer a second nail two inches from the opposite end in line with nail number 2. Continue

DEMONSTRATING THE SPEED OF SOUND WAVES

This experiment requires a length of metal at least seventy-five-feet long. An iron fence will have continuous rods running through it or a roll of wire can be stretched the length of your backyard or school ground. Be sure it is taut. Stand at one end, with a partner at the opposite end holding two rocks. Place your ear very close to the wire or rod while your friend strikes the rocks together with the metal trapped between. Listen closely for two sounds—one following immediately after the other. The sound is coming through the air as well as through the metal. Do sound waves move faster in a gas or a solid?

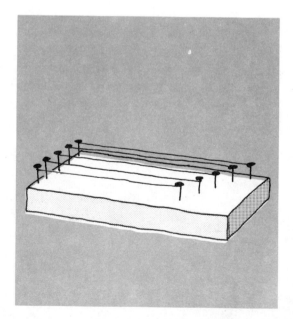

placing nails number 3, 4, and 5 two inches in from each preceding nail. Find five strong rubber bands of the same size and length. Cut each band. Tie one end to a nail and the other end to the nail at the opposite end. Pluck each rubber band. What have you learned about pitch?

You can vary the above by placing a row of nails along both ends of a board, the same distance apart but close enough to stretch a rubber band around opposing nails without cutting the bands. Select five rubber bands that are the same length but vary in width. String the bands and then pluck away. What can you say about pitch with this setup?

Another experiment with a vibrating column of air requires only a large drinking straw and a pair of scissors. Cut diagonally across the end of one of the straws. Hold this end rather loosely between your lips and blow into the straw. You may have to experiment quite a bit with cutting straws before you produce a good straw. When you are able to make a sound, either cut finger holes in the length of the straw in the manner of a clarinet or chop pieces off the end of the straw with the scissors as you blow. How does the length of the straw affect the pitch?

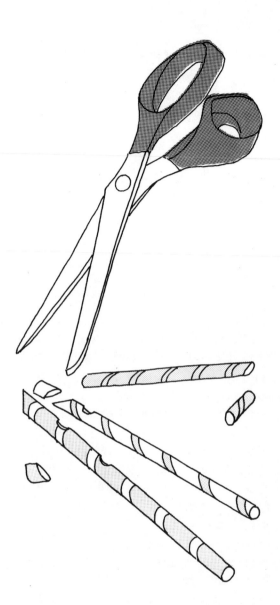

Chapter 6
Color and Light

MAKING A SPECTRUM

Make a slit (1″ X ½″) in a sheet of cardboard and tape it to a sunny window. Hold a prism close to the slit so that the beam of light hits one angle of the prism. If the walls in the room are white they can be used to see the spectrum. If not, set up a screen or large poster board. Light waves are bent or refracted as they go through the prism. Violet is bent the most and red the least. List the order of colors in between. What can you say about white light? Can you take the spectrum and converge it back into white light? Try a magnifying glass. How do raindrops and sunlight cause a rainbow? What are the positions of these two factors in relation to where you are standing when you see a rainbow?

Use the same setup above to check out the temperature variance in a spectrum. Direct the sunlight going through the prism to a thermometer so that only the violet color hits the bulb for several minutes. Record the temperature. Move the prism slightly so the indigo color shines on the bulb for several minutes. Continue this procedure through all the colors of the spectrum. Graph the temperature readings and draw conclusions.

DEFINITIONS

prism — a wedge-shaped piece of transparent material, frequently glass, that refracts white light passing through it to give a continuous spectrum.

spectrum — the colored bands of light produced by passing white or other complex light through a prism or diffraction grating, progressing from the longest visible wave length (red) to the shortest (violet).

SPINNING COLORS

Cut a six-inch disk of cardboard. Mark off three pie-shaped pieces. Paint one section red, one green, and the third one blue. Push the end of a round pencil into the center and tape it in place. Hold the pencil between the palms of the hands and spin the disk as fast as possible. You can also attach the disk to the end of a power drill or electric beater. What color do you see?

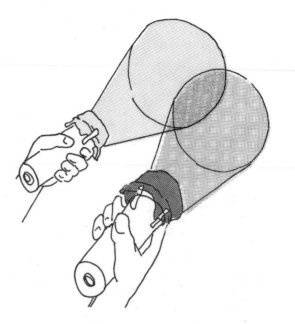

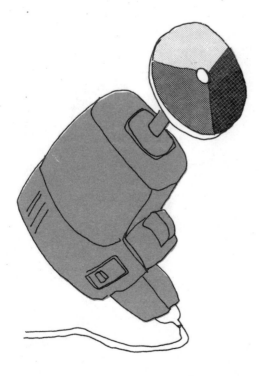

MIXING COLORED LIGHTS

Obtain three flashlights. Cover the front end of each with a different colored piece of cellophane. Try red, yellow, and blue. Tape each piece securely in place.

Project the red and yellow lights on a white poster board or wall in a dark room or closet. Overlay the lights in the center. What color does it make? Try other combinations and record. Shoot the light from all three flashlights on the same spot. What color do you get? Would you get the same results if you used water colors or paint instead of light?

65

TESTING THE EFFECT OF COLORED LIGHTS ON PLANT GROWTH

Plant several seeds of the same kind in a number of paper cups. Use the same type of soil for each planter and give each the same amount of water. Make cones out of cellophane paper so that the base of a cone just slips over the top of a paper cup. Use cellophane tape to anchor the cones to the cups after seeds have been planted and watered. Use cones of red, yellow, green, blue, and black. Observe the rate of germination, rate of growth, color of leaves, and sturdiness of stems as the seedlings grow under each of the colors. What can you conclude?

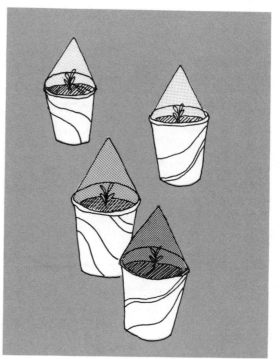

SEEING THE COLORS OF AN OIL SPILL

Fill an aluminum foil pan one-half full of water. Make a dark solution by spraying or mixing in black latex paint. Place the pan in a bright, shady place, not in full sunlight. While looking at the black mixture in a position that reflects light to you, pour a little vegetable oil on the surface nearest you. Watch the oil spread over the surface. Describe what colors you see.

TESTING
COLOR ABSORPTION

For this test you will need a flashlight, pieces of different colored cellophane, and a box of crayons. Fasten a piece of red cellophane over the end of a flashlight. With a friend go into a very dark room. Select a crayon, one color at a time, and direct the light from the flashlight on it. Repeat with the other crayons, each time recording its color and the color it appears in the light through the red cellophane. Repeat the process with blue and yellow cellophane. Can you draw conclusions about absorption of colors?

PLAYING WITH MIRRORS

Set a large mirror at an angle in an aquarium of water. This should not disturb the fish too much. Shine a bright light into the mirror. The beam from a slide projector works well. Darken the room. Move the light source until the reflected light hits the ceiling or wall. What did the mirror do to white light?

Take a mirror into a sunny room where a beam of sunlight is hitting an object on one side of the room. Use the mirror to direct the rays of light onto an object across the room. Find a couple of friends and give them each a mirror. Make the rays bounce off one mirror to the second mirror, then time how long it takes the third person to direct this light to a given object. What does this prove about angles of reflection?

Tape two mirrors together and set them upright on a flat surface like an open book. Put various objects in front and observe the numbers and positions reflected to you. Vary the angle of the mirrors.

Polish a sheet of metal until you can see yourself in it. Bend it slightly to form a curve as in a concave lens. Look at yourself. Bend it the other way as in a convex lens. How do you look now? Some restaurants and amusement parks have mirrors shaped this way so that one looks either tall and skinny or short and fat.

Turn your back on a roomful of people. Use a mirror to locate a friend. After a few tries you can figure out the angle of reflection and incidence and locate a person quickly and efficiently.

DEFINITIONS

concave — curved in.

convex — curved out.

WORKING WITH CONCAVE AND CONVEX LENSES

Lenses can be purchased or obtained from discarded eyeglasses or other optical devices. A lens that curves out to the sides is called convex. One that curves in to the center is a concave lens.

Bend the bottom of a sheet of cardboard so that it stands upright on a table. Set a lighted candle in a holder about a foot away from the cardboard. Hold a convex lens between the two objects so that the burning candle appears on the cardboard. Vary the position of the lens from close to the cardboard to close to the candle. How does the image change? Try it now with a concave lens.

Hold a convex lens in a window of sunshine. Direct the sun's rays to a spot on a surface until you are the right distance to get the brightest light. This is the focal point for your convex lens and the distance can be measured. What does a convex lens or magnifying glass do with light rays? Use a concave lens. Can you measure a focal point for it?

Take your two lenses and look through them at objects in a room. Are things ever upside down? Blurry? Larger? Smaller? Which type would a person need if he or she were nearsighted? Farsighted?

DETERMINING HOW LIGHT TRAVELS

Cut a hole through the middle of three pieces of cardboard or some other stiff paper. Bend the pieces an inch from the bottom. Stand them upright about a foot apart on a table, placed so they are in a straight line. Can you see straight through the holes? Light a candle and place it at the end of the table opposite from where you are standing. Look through the holes to see if the candle can be seen. Move one of the pieces to one side. What happens? What does this tell you about the direction in which light travels?

CALCULATING THE MAGNITUDE OF LENSES

Collect a variety of lenses: reading glasses, old spectacles, eyepieces from microscopes, lenses from old movie and slide projectors, binoculars, cameras, and opera glasses. If you take a lens from a usable instrument be sure to remove it carefully and remember how to return it to its proper position.

Obtain a sheet of graph paper or use a ruler and make equidistant lines. Hold an eyepiece from a microscope over the paper and bring it into focus. Count the number of lines you see through it in relation to the number of lines seen outside the lens. For example, if there are ten lines outside to one on the inside the power of the eyepiece is 10X. Test all the lenses to determine their magnifying power.

PREVENTING REFLECTION OF LIGHT

In a darkened room shine a light into the top of a jar of clear water. Notice how bright it is in the water yet the outside is dark. Add a few drops of milk to the water and stir the solution. Shine the light into the jar again. This time how does the light inside the jar compare to that outside the jar?

In the clear water the light hits the jar at such a small angle that total reflection occurs. By adding other particles to the water the light hits these and is reflected through the glass.

TESTING LIGHT ABSORPTION

Cover a thermometer with a black cloth. Cover a second thermometer with a white cloth. Set both covered thermometers in the sun for one-half hour. Which one then registers a higher temperature? Does the black or white cloth absorb more light and therefore more heat?

If you can find two plastic containers (like those used to hold leftover food), you can do an even more dramatic experiment. Paint one container black and one white. Place both under a strong light, preferably a heat lamp. After a few minutes you will see a change occur in one of the containers. What happens? Why?

EXPERIMENTING
WITH REFRACTION

Put a coin in the bottom of a coffee can. Stand so that you can see the coin. Now move slowly back so the coin just barely disappears from sight. Stop. Have a friend pour water slowly and carefully into the can so that the coin is not moved. The coin will suddenly come into your sight again.

Set a pencil or stick into a glass almost full of water. Stand back and view the object from the side of the glass at water level. Explain its appearance now.

Cut a hole in a cylinder of cardboard. Tape this over the end of a flashlight. Shine the beam at an angle down into a glass of water. What happens to the light rays as it starts through the liquid?

Light waves bend and change direction (refract) when they go from one material, such as air, to another kind of material, such as water. The speeds at which light waves travel through air and water are different.

EXPERIMENTING WITH REFLECTION

Using a smoke box is the best way to study light. You can build a smoke box that shows how light is reflected or refracted and how lenses work.

Make a wooden box. Panes of glass cut to fit should be put in the front and top and taped in place. Remove the back wall of the box and cover it with black cloth, hung like a curtain. Make the curtain in two overlapping sections so you can easily put your hand in the box. Tack the cloth to the sides and tape it to the glass top. Cut a window in one end of the box, about three inches from the glass front. The window should be about 3½ inches long by 2½ inches wide. It will be covered with an index card with various shaped holes in it, depending on the experiment you are doing.

Cut three holes in a card, the same distance from each other and one-fourth inch in diameter. Set a container of burning incense or punk inside the box to produce smoke. Focus a flashlight on the three-hole card by moving it back and forth until the rays are well defined in the smoke. Hold a mirror in the box at a 45° angle from the floor of the box. What is the condition of the reflected rays?

To see the contrast with reflection from a rough surface, rough a piece of cellophane with sandpaper or steel wool and fasten it to a piece of glass. How does this affect the way the rays of light are reflected? Hold a piece of wood in the path of the light rays. Are they reflected? Try other surfaces.

DEFINITIONS

reflect — to throw back an image.

refract — to cause a sound wave or light wave to change direction when they pass through an object of another density.

Chapter 7
Heat

FINDING THE KINDLING TEMPERATURE OF MATERIALS

Place an unwaxed paper cup half full of water on a hot plate. Turn the dial to medium heat. Take the temperature of the water periodically until it reaches the boiling point. Is the paper cup still holding up? Keep boiling the water until it has changed to vapor. Now what happens to the cup? Is the kindling temperature of paper lower or higher than the temperature at which water boils?

Set a metal pie pan on a hot plate or other source of heat. Place small pieces of the following materials of near equal size in the pan: charcoal, wood, cotton cloth, newsprint, solder, paraffin, iron nail, eraser, plastic, wax paper, aluminum foil. Heat these objects for half an hour. Which one reaches its kindling temperature first? Remember to use very small pieces. How hot a fire would you need to melt the nail? Research the process used in steel mills, welding shops, and similar industries.

What is the kindling temperature of liquids—the point at which they boil? Use small aluminum cups or Pyrex dishes to heat some liquids. Use two tablespoons of each for this experiment. Use a candy thermometer to check the temperatures. Locate the kindling point of water, milk, rubbing alcohol, sugar solution, vegetable oil, detergent, and other common household liquids that are safe to boil. Graph the thermometer reading and time to reach the kindling temperature for each liquid. How can you explain the difference?

TESTING FOR HEAT CONDUCTIVITY

With tongs, hold one end of a metal rod. Place the other end in the flame of a candle. Touch the rod. Will a solid, such as metal, carry heat? Fill a Pyrex bottle with cold water. Place it over a Bunsen burner or on an electric hot plate. After five minutes feel the top part of the bottle. Will liquids, such as the water in the bottle, carry heat? In the winter hold your hand above a radiator. What do you feel? Does air, a gas, carry heat?

Fasten a wire to two upright posts high enough to place a candle under it. Warm up a hunk of paraffin in order to break off small pieces. Mold little balls of it around the wire. Space the paraffin at equal intervals along the wire. Heat one end of the wire and time the rate at which the balls of paraffin melt and drop off.

Test the conductivity of different solids. Locate several rods of approximately the same size: wooden dowel, brass curtain rod, iron, plastic, and glass. In a coffee can punch holes large enough so that rubber stoppers fit tightly in them. If you have no rubber stoppers, use corks with holes through them. Insert the rods through the holes in the stoppers and fit the rods and stoppers into the can. Now put a small piece of paraffin on the end of each rod. Fill the can with very hot water. Do the pieces of paraffin fall off at the same time? What does this tell you about the rates at which metals and other solids conduct heat? Which is the best conductor?

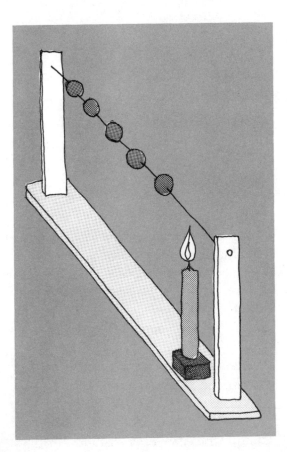

TRANSFERRING HEAT BY RADIATION

Heat radiates by electromagnetic waves. These waves move faster than when heat is transferred by convection or conduction. Try these activities to help you understand the principle of heat by radiation.

Hold your hand near a toaster or iron that has been turned on.

Place a sheet of paper outside on the sidewalk on a sunny day. Use a magnifying glass or convex lens to focus the sun's radiant energy on a single focal point on the paper. What happens?

Stand in front of a window through which the sun is shining. Can you feel the heat?

Tape black felt around one pop bottle, sandpaper around a second one, and leave the third bottle uncovered (clear glass). Set a thermometer in each one and place them in the sun. Every five minutes for half an hour take temperature readings in each container. Now bring the bottles into an air-conditioned room. Read the temperatures again every five minutes. Which absorbed heat by radiation the fastest? The slowest? Which was the first to lose heat by radiation? Which was last?

DEFINITIONS

conduction — the process of carrying or transmitting.

convection — the flow of heat from one place to another, caused by convection current (mass movements of heated particles) in liquids and gases.

IDENTIFYING THE GAS NECESSARY FOR FIRES

Collect five candles of the same diameter. Locate four jars or bottles: a half-pint, pint, quart, and a two-quart. Use a lighted match to heat the bottom of each candle. Set them on a cake pan far enough apart so that the jars will not touch when placed over the candles. Light one candle and do not cover it. It will be the control. Light a second candle and cover it with the half-pint. Using a stopwatch or a clock with a second hand, time how long the candle burns before it goes out. Repeat the procedure with the other jars. Do you see any pattern to your findings?

Atmosphere or air has about 78 percent nitrogen, 21 percent oxygen, and 1 percent other gases. To check out which gas the candle flames were using before they burned out, repeat the above experiment. This time fill the cake pan at least half full of water. Relight a candle and place a jar over it. As the candle burns and goes out water comes into the jar. Figure out the percentage of rise in the jar. Repeat the process with the other candles and jars. What gas was used up as materials burned?

EXPERIMENTING WITH CONTRACTION AND EXPANSION

Pull the mouth of a small balloon over the opening of an empty (except for air) test tube. Using a test-tube holder place the tube over a candle flame. What happens to the balloon?

A commercial ball and ring can be used for this experiment, or a home-made device can be assembled with a hook eye and screw. The hook eye can be adjusted so the screw just slips through the eye of the hook. With tongs, hold the screw over the flame of a candle for a few minutes. Try to insert it through the opening in the hook eye. What happens to it?

Fill a glass three-fourths full of water. Use a grease pencil or piece of tape to mark the exact level of the liquid. Set the glass in a freezer overnight. Remeasure the level. Does freezing cause water to contract or expand?

Collect a number of small bottles with small openings at the top. Mold balls of modeling clay around one end of plastic straws that can be inserted, airtight, into the neck of the bottles. Fill each bottle with a different liquid: oil, water, concentrated salt solution, molasses, rubbing alcohol, etc. Stopper the bottles with the clay holding the straws upright. Set all bottles in the same pan of water and heat on a hot plate. (Never heat alcohol over an open flame even if it is confined in a bottle.) Every five minutes measure the height of each liquid. What factor affects the rate and degree of expansion?

Blow up a balloon. With a string measure the circumference of the balloon. Stretch the string along a ruler to translate the size into inches. Place the balloon in a refrigerator for five minutes. Remeasure. Place it in a freezer for five minutes. Remeasure. How does temperature affect the contraction of a gas?

DEMONSTRATING CONVECTION IN LIQUIDS

Fill one vinegar or pop bottle with cold water that has been in a refrigerator overnight. Fill a second one with hot water colored with vegetable dye or ink. Hold a piece of heavy cardboard over the mouth of the cold bottle and turn it upside down. Place it exactly over the mouth of the hot bottle and then carefully slip out the cardboard. Observe the movement of the liquids. Which one is heavier? Repeat the experiment, but this time put the hot bottle on top. How does it react now? How does this explain the temperature of lakes at different depths?

Is heat always the factor in the movement between two liquids? Repeat the experiment, using one bottle with water and the other one with oil. Then try oil and vinegar. Use smaller bottles with these solutions or figure out a way to use them after the experiment so as to conserve materials.

CHANGING ELECTRICAL ENERGY INTO HEAT ENERGY

Remove the insulation from both ends and a center section of a piece of bell wire. Connect the ends to the terminals of a 1½ volt dry cell. Place a finger on the bare wire in the center of the circle. Does it feel warm? (Do not leave it connected too long as it wears down the dry cell.)

Examine various appliances and devices in the home and school where electricity is changed to heat: electric blanket, heating pad, toaster, steam iron, water heater, fuses, curling iron, soldering iron, and electric stove.

Briefly touch a 40-watt light bulb that has been burning for a while. Now touch a 100-watt bulb. Turn off the lights and examine the filaments inside. Why do some bulbs give off more light and more heat?

COLORING FIREWOOD

Collect small pieces of dry wood. Softwoods, such as pine and cottonwood, are better than hardwoods, such as oak and maple. You will need a number of chemicals that can be purchased at a drugstore, nursery, or science supply house. Most junior high school labs also have a supply of chemicals. One-fourth pound of each is enough for this experiment. Mix one chemical at a time into a quart of water in an old jar or can. Put in the pieces of wood and let them soak for two days. Use prongs to set them out to dry. Do not get any of the chemicals on your hands or clothes. Bottle up the remaining solutions for later use.

When these pieces of wood are burned in a fireplace, they give off the colors of the rainbow. The following list gives the flame colors for some chemicals: copper chloride, greenish blue; potassium chloride, purple; strontium nitrate, reddish; barium nitrate, green. A chemistry teacher may have suggestions of other chemicals to use. **Never** burn an unknown chemical compound without checking with an expert in the field.

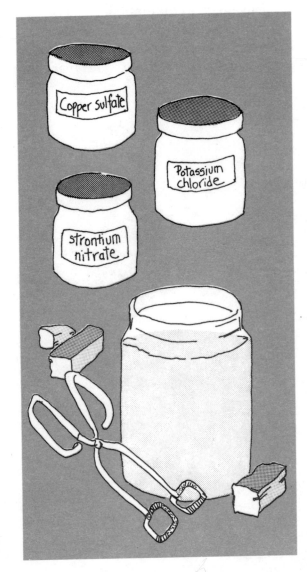

SEEKING ANSWERS TO HOT PROBLEMS

Some of the knotty questions below can be answered if you design experiments to solve them. Others can be solved by setting up several hypotheses and then reasoning them out. As a last resort turn to encyclopedias and other library sources to find the answers.

Why do many automobile owners put more air in tires during cold weather?

Why are sidewalks and highways made with cracks or separations at various intervals?

Why do people in the winter wear dark rather than light-colored clothes, often made of wool rather than cotton?

Why can't you pop sweet or field corn as you can popcorn?

What causes water vapor to collect or "steam up" on windows?

Why do most cooking and frying pans have handles of Bakelite or wood?

Why will a match ignite if struck on sandpaper but not if struck on glass?

In the summer why is it cooler near a lake than farther inland?

How does a thermostat kick a furnace on and off?

What happens when you "blow a fuse"?

Appendix

Chapter 1

COMPARING GASES page 11

The balloon filled with a higher concentration of carbon dioxide will reach the ground first. Air is a mixture of gases: 78 percent nitrogen, 21 percent oxygen, .03 percent carbon dioxide, and less than 1 percent other gases, unless the atmosphere is polluted.

CHANGING A LIQUID TO A GAS page 12

The solutions in the closed containers will remain in solution. In the saucers the water evaporates, leaving behind either crystals or powder of the solid that was dissolved in the water.

CHANGING A LIQUID TO A SOLID page 13

Concrete is usually a mixture of cement, clay, limestone, and water. When the liquid evaporates, the remaining materials harden.

Sugar is obtained from cane stems or beet roots. Salt crystals can be removed from ocean water. Numerous industries extract solids from liquids.

CHANGING A SOLID TO A GAS page 14

Dry ice is frozen carbon dioxide. A concentration of this gas will surround the flame of the match. Since this reduces the amount of oxygen, the match will go out.

Appendix

PRODUCING OXYGEN page 17

Oxygen is a necessary element for fire and is produced in this chemical reaction of hydrogen peroxide and charcoal. The match or splint should ignite again and continue to burn.

EXPERIMENTING
WITH OXIDATION   page 18

The steel wool will turn brownish. The common name for iron oxide is rust. The water will rise about one fifth the way inside the jar. Air has around 21 percent oxygen.

The glowing splint will get brighter as oxygen is released in this chemical reaction.

REPLACING METALS page 19

Copper will collect on the iron screws. Aluminum plus oxygen produces aluminum oxide. Some metals react with water and replace some of the hydrogen. Hydroxides are formed as hydrogen is given off.

MAKING NEW MATERIALS
FROM OLD   page 20

Carbon is formed on burned bread. Vinegar coagulates milk. Sulfur and silver combine to form silver sulfide. Iron and oxygen form iron oxide or rust. Caramel forms as sugar is heated. A homemade ink is made from water, iron sulfate, and tannic acid.

MAKING AN EMULSION   page 20

Bits of string will float in a glass of water. The string will settle to the bottom of the water with detergent added. Particles on soiled clothes are washed away when soap is added to a washing machine.

Soon after shaking, the oil and vinegar will separate, the oil floating on top of the vinegar. Egg white causes the oil to break into small droplets that stay scattered throughout the vinegar.

Bile works the same way as the egg white in the previous experiment.

PROVING MOLECULAR MOTION   page 24

All four solids will gradually dissolve. Molecules of liquids and gases are constantly moving around. Any solid that will dissolve in a liquid is soon spread by diffusion.

CALCULATING THE SPECIFIC GRAVITY OF MATERIALS   page 24

Mercury, the heaviest liquid, will settle to the bottom. Water is next and the oil floats on top of it. The coin will drop to the mercury. The heavy wood drops to the water and the lightweight balsa floats on the oil.

Specific gravity is the relationship between the density of a liquid to that of water.

CHECKING THE BUOYANCY OF FLUIDS   page 25

An object will sink if it weighs more than the water it displaces. An object will float if it weighs the same or less than the volume of water it displaces.

The shape and volume of an object affects buoyancy. A wad of aluminum foil will sink and a sheet will float.

The density of a liquid affects the buoyancy force on objects in it. Salt water is denser than fresh water. It is easier to float in an ocean than in a fresh water lake.

SEPARATING MIXTURES   page 26

The sand and salt are not chemically combined for the white and beige crystals are still obvious. Pouring water over the mixture will cause the salt to dissolve. Pour off the water in a shallow pan and leave it for several days. Water evaporates, leaving salt crystals.

A magnet attracts iron, steel, nickel, and cobalt. It will pick up the filings and buckshot. The sugar and cork remain.

SEPARATING COMPOUNDS page 27

Amylase is the enzyme in saliva that starts the digestion of carbohydrates.

Burning will separate sugar into carbon and water.

The carbon in the candle collects on the bottom of the pan.

INVESTIGATING THE SOLUBILITY OF COMPOUNDS page 28

Water is the best solvent and all compounds in the experiment, except vegetable oil, will dissolve in it. Some dissolve easier than others. The same is true of vinegar, milk, and lemon juice. Alcohol is the only one that works with oil.

Chapter 2

WORKING WITH FIXED AND MOVABLE PULLEYS page 32

The effort to raise a weight on a fixed pulley is slightly more than the weight of the object since there is friction between the cord and pulley. The advantage is a change in direction of the force. The amount of force needed and the speed or the distance traveled are not reduced by using a fixed pulley.

A movable pulley should cut your work or effort in half if the pulley is well lubricated.

WORKING WITH WEDGES page 33

Wedges found in the kitchen or garage would be a knife, the cutting wheel on a can opener, blades on a meat grinder and eggbeater, teeth on a saw, and blades on a router, chisel, hoe, and spade.

A long tapering wedge requires less effort than a short blunt one. It will take more blows or longer time to drive it into the ground.

DEMONSTRATING THE PRINCIPLE OF A SCREW page 34

The more threads on a screw the easier it is to get it into the wood. It will take many more turns of the screwdriver before the job is done.

Lubricating the screw will cut down on the amount of friction between the wood and metal.

CLASSIFYING LEVER ACTION   page 36

1.	1	10.	3
2.	3	11.	3
3.	1	12.	2
4.	3	13.	2
5.	3	14.	2
6.	3	15.	1
7.	3	16.	3
8.	2	17.	2
9.	1		

CALCULATING MECHANICAL ADVANTAGE OF LEVERS   page 37

The mechanical advantage (MA) of 40 grams balancing 120 grams is three.

In the second problem 100 grams two inches from the fulcrum needs 50 grams four inches on the other side of the fulcrum in order to balance.

The closer the resistance is to the fulcrum the less effort needed to lift it.

EXPERIMENTING WITH MASS AND MOMENTUM   page 40

Mass is the actual quantity of matter in an object. Weight is also quantity of matter, but it varies depending whether you are in Miami or on the moon. Mass is constant. The golf ball has greater mass than the Ping-Pong ball. Momentum equals the mass of the body times its velocity. An object with greater mass, once set in motion, will go faster and farther.

UNDERSTANDING INERTIA   page 41

The principle of inertia states that an object at rest tends to stay at rest even when some force is trying to move it. It also states that an object that is moving tends to keep moving, resisting effort to stop it.

WORKING WITH GEARS   page 42

The wheels will rotate in opposite directions. The two-inch wheel will rotate twice to each single rotation of the four-inch wheel.

A gear will carry or transmit energy so that one moving part makes other parts move. It can change the direction of motion and increase or decrease rotation.

DEMONSTRATING BERNOULLI'S PRINCIPLE   page 43

The stream of air is small and fast. The pressure between the balls is lowered, causing them to attract one another.

Blowing over a paper causes it to move up. Since the air is moving faster the molecules are farther apart than those on the underside. The greater pressure on the bottom of a wing gives it the lift.

Chapter 3

PRODUCING A CHARGE WITH FRICTION   page 44

1. You become electrically charged when you shuffle your rubber-soled shoes on a wool rug. As you touch a metal object sparks will fly as your body quickly becomes discharged.

2. When you comb the fur of a cat or your own hair, the comb picks up electrons leaving the individual hairs with a positive charge. They repel each other and the hairs stand out.

3. The balloon becomes negatively charged. When it touches a neutral wall, the electrons in it move in to give it a positive charge on the surface. The balloon is attracted and sticks to the wall.

4. The glass rod becomes positively charged and causes the stream of water to be attracted.

5. The negatively charged balloon will cause a faint glow in the fluorescent tube for a second or two.

6. The sheet of paper will become charged and cling to the wall temporarily.

7. The positively charged glass cover attracts the paper. As soon as the paper touches the glass, the paper gives up electrons to the glass and is also positively charged. The paper then drops, for like charges repel.

IDENTIFYING SOLIDS THAT WILL CONDUCT ELECTRICITY   page 47

Conductors include iron, steel, tin, copper, silver, zinc, aluminum, and carbon.

Nonconductors are paper, cloth, wood, stone, most plastic, glass, rubber, cork, and porcelain.

Appendix

USING SALT TO CONDUCT ELECTRICITY   page 48

Pure water will not conduct electricity. Adding salt to water provides an electrolyte solution. The more salt you add, the brighter the light until you have a saturated solution. This gives a light as bright as you can achieve with this electrolyte. Salt contains negatively charged chloride and positively charged sodium ions. A stream of electrons flows from the chloride to the sodium ions.

DEMONSTRATING THE FUNCTION OF A FUSE page 50

The electricity flowing through three dry cells in series produces enough heat to melt the foil fuse. When a circuit is overloaded with lights and/or appliances, the heat melts the thin metal strip in a screw-type fuse in the electrical box.

The newer type fuse, a circuit breaker, will break the flow of electrons when the wire becomes too hot. It can be reset when part of the load on the circuit is reduced.

Index

Index

Index

Helen J. Challand earned her M.A. and Ph.D. from Northwestern University. She currently is Chair of the Science Department at National College of Education and Coordinator of Undergraduate Studies for the college's West Suburban Campus.

An experienced classroom teacher and science consultant, Dr. Challand has worked on science projects for Scott Foresman and Company, Rand McNally Publishers, Harper-Row Publishers, Encyclopedia Britannica Films, Coronet Films, and Journal Films. She is associate editor for the *Young People's Science Encyclopedia* published by Childrens Press.